How We M Around

Text: **Núria Roca**

Illustrations: **Rosa M. Curto**

BARRON'S

Little children, when they are so little they are called babies, walk on **all fours.**
But not all babies, because some prefer to crawl!

Have your parents ever told you how you went
from one place to another when you were a baby?

There are many animals that walk on **four legs,** like babies. Some are huge, like elephants, and others are so small they would fit in your pocket, like mice.

Do you know any other animals that walk on four legs

When babies grow up, they learn to walk on **two legs.** At first they have trouble standing up, but with practice all of them end up learning how to walk. There are children who cannot stand up and need crutches or a wheelchair to go from one place to another. Do you need any of these things?

Now close your eyes and think about animals that walk on **two legs,** like grown children. 1, 2, 3!
Can you name some?

Kangaroos, dinosaurs, penguins, hens…and all birds

walk on two legs! Can you think of any other**?**

There are animals with not a single leg, like snakes.

Most snakes are so easily frightened that they

crawl away through the grass when they

hear someone getting near.

Earthworms have no legs. And they don't have

eyes either! They don't need them because

they live underground.

There are some small animals that have so many legs and so tiny that it would be very difficult to count them. They are the **millipedes** and **centipedes,** which look like worms with legs.

Can you imagine if they had to wear shoes?

Do you like **spiders**? Some are poisonous, like some snakes, but most of them are harmless. If you watch one in its cobweb, you will be able to count how many legs it has.

If not, you may count the legs of the spider on the opposite page. It has … 1, 2, 3, 4, 5, 6, 7, and 8 legs. That's a lot!

There are many, many animals,
but the most abundant ones, the
ones of which there are more than
any other kind, are **insects:**
ladybugs, bees, ants, butterflies…
and they all have SIX LEGS!
So small yet so important!

It is small, red with black polka dots, it walks on six legs but it also has wings… and it may fly! It is called a **ladybug,** and it loves looking for food in plants.

Since it is red, you can see it very well when it walks among the leaves.

Ladybugs are red-colored,
so they stand out when they
walk through the leaves in
search of food.

Guess what insect flies from one flower to the next, has black and yellow stripes, makes delicious honey, and may sting you if you bother it. It's the **bee!**

Can you count how many legs it has?

And have you seen how pretty their honeycombs are?

Some tiny animals, such as the **ants,** walk
underground and only come out of their anthill
to look for food. If one of them walks on your arm,
it will tickle you!
And there are others that live inside all kinds of wood,
where they make tunnels: they are called termites.

Have you ever seen a dog with **fleas?** They are very tiny insects that hide in the fur of the animals and eat by sucking their blood.

Fleas, lice,
and mosquitoes

bite people. They have one, two,

three, four, five, six legs, and they

are nasty!

There are many **animals**
such as frogs, birds or anteaters
that look around for insects they like
to eat. Some walk or jump, others
fly or swim under the water.
There are many ways to move
from one place to another!

There are some animals that live far away from our homes and others that live inside them. Some, like **butterflies** and **dragonflies,** are so colorful that illustrators love drawing them in stories.

We share our planet with a lot of animals, some with many legs and some with no legs at all.

A die with many legs

For this game you need a die. To make one, just duplicate this drawing on a piece of cardboard and cut it out. Then fold each square until you make a die. Put some glue on the little white strips sticking out of squares 2, 5, and 6, and press them gently against the sides of the squares so the die doesn't crumple. When you are done, the game may begin.

The players should sit on the floor making a circle. Taking turns, each player throws the die and then has to name an animal with the same number of legs as the number that appears on top of the die. Repeating names is not allowed! The player who gets number 1, 3, or 5 just keeps quiet and passes the die on to the next player. The player who can't think of any animal will have to do whatever the other players demand, like singing, dancing, jumping, and so forth. Good luck!

**Remember:
You can't use the
same name twice!**

A flying butterfly

Would you like to make a butterfly that flies? Well, go ahead then. All you need is a drinking straw, some tracing paper, some regular paper, cardboard in different colors, a pair of scissors, a bit of glue… and the help of a grown-up!

1. Trace the templates for the butterfly and for the reinforcement. Cut out the cardboard with these templates.
2. Punch a hole in the middle of the reinforcement. Now wrap a strip of paper 1½ inches long around the drinking straw and glue the end so as to make a tube. (Be careful not to glue the paper to the straw.)
3. Insert the tip of the tube you have made through the hole in the reinforcement. Make two little cuts in the tube and glue the flaps to the reinforcement.
4. Decorate the wings as you like and glue the butterfly to the reinforcement.
5. Introduce the drinking straw inside the paper tube that holds the wings.
Now the butterfly is ready to fly! Hold the straw with the palms of both hands and make it roll back and forth, then shoot it into the air with a sudden twist of the hands. If you bend the tip of the wings slightly upward, your butterfly will fly better.

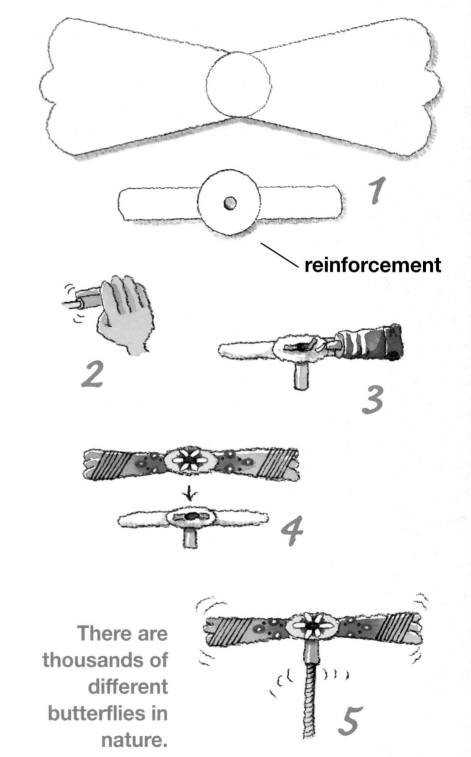

reinforcement

There are thousands of different butterflies in nature.

A window full of insects

If you want to see insects every day, make this funny curtain. You just need some cardboard in different colors, a sewing needle, some thread, a pencil, a pair of scissors, the will to draw, and the help from a grown-up.

Draw as many insects as you wish, cut them out, and paint them in funny colors. You may use red cardboard for ladybugs, yellow for wasps, orange for butterflies, green for beetles… This way you will only have to color one part of the insect!

Once you have all the insects you want, use a needle and thread to make the strings of the curtain. Tie a knot on either end of each insect so it will remain tightly in place. Make as many strings as you want and, when you are done, hang them on the windowpane. Use adhesive tape or the kind of glue that can be easily wiped clean later.

Do you remember how many legs insects have?

Hopscotch!

Draw a rectangle on the ground and divide it into six boxes. Add a bigger rectangle at the top, as shown in the drawing.

To start the game, drop a pebble inside the first box, leave it there, and jump on one foot from one box to the next until you get to the rest spot on the top box. Here you may stand on both feet and rest for a while. You also have to jump all the way back on one foot. When you get to box number one, pick up the pebble, always hopping on one foot, and jump out of the drawing on the ground. Now it is another player's turn. When all the players have done number 1, you start with number 2 and go over the whole process again until everybody has covered the six boxes. When a player steps on a line or puts both feet on the ground, he or she has to leave, wait for her next turn and do the failed number again.

Your parents should know this game well. Ask them!

Rest

6
5
4
3
2
1

Here are some games you may play with your friends. The only thing you have to do is walk. The first game is **Walking very slowly**. Take very long steps, lifting each leg as high as you can. The winner is the last one to arrive! Next comes **Walking while sitting**. All the players sit on the floor, with their legs straight in front and the trunk at a square angle. The game consists of moving forward using your buttocks as if they were feet. Now, all can **Walk on all fours**, as when you were babies. Play the game moving forward or backward, and see who's the fastest.

A line is formed in **Going after the king**, and the first kid is the king. Everybody must walk behind and repeat everything the king does. Finally, with a **foot tied up**, all the players stand by twos and tie up their left foot to the right foot of the other player. Who will be the first two to get to the finishing line? If one of the players falls down, both of them have to start all over again, so you'd better watch out!

Note to parents

Learning how to walk

Children like to be told how they learned to walk. For most toddlers, vertical locomotion starts between the ages of 10 and 18 months. It is a very intense period for them. When they are older, it is interesting to talk to them about how they started going from one place to another. Did they go on all fours? Did they drag themselves on their little buttocks?

When babies start to walk, they usually do it on unsteady feet, which leads to many anecdotes they love to hear over and over again. The first and second chapters may be used so the children may recall their "first steps," not only those their parents remember, but also the ones remembered by all the people in the family. There are many children who cannot walk. Some have never been able to, while others lost the ability to do it due to an accident or some crippling disease. It is important to talk about all these possibilities and have the children suggest ideas that maybe you have overlooked: temporary crutches, wheelchairs, walking canes, and so on. Keep the conversation within commonsense standards, whether your child has a disability or not.

Going to and from

Animals may go from one place to another in different ways. Some may fly in the air, others swim in the water, and still others move on the ground, like human beings do. Animals may walk or crawl, walk on two legs like we do, on four legs like lions, on six legs like insects, on eight legs like spiders, or on more than ten legs, like centipedes. Many people think spiders are insects, but spiders have eight legs and that means they are not insects. The best way to define an insect and separate it from any other animal is counting its legs, although this is not always easy.

Facts about insects

Insects are very different from us, so much so that many films about aliens have used insects as their models. In fact, insects are the most numerous animals on earth. The figure is 10 trillion insects alive, compared to approximately 6 billion humans. You may find insects everywhere, from the hottest deserts to inside our homes, and they have a big influence in our daily life. Many people strongly dislike insects. There are some insects that bite, transmit diseases, destroy crops or affect furniture, but most of them are useful little animals. They help pollination and also keep plagues in check. If insects disappeared, the world would not be as we know it.

A famous riddle, and a couple more

Kids love riddles and here we suggest a few.

One of them is the famous enigma of the Thebes Sphinx, mentioned in the Greek tragedy of Oedipus. The sphinx devoured anyone who could not correctly answer the following enigma: Which animal has four legs in the morning, two legs at noon, three at night, and the more legs it has, the weaker it is? It is a better idea to present this riddle to the younger children like this: Which animal walks on four legs when it is born, on two legs when it is an adult, and on three legs when it is old? "It is man," answered Oedipus. "When he is born, he walks on all four (four legs), when he is a grown-up he stands up (two legs), and when he is old he needs the help of a walking stick (three legs)." When the sphinx heard the correct answer, it destroyed itself and left Thebes free of terror.

Here are some easier riddles:

Which animal has six legs but always goes on four? The flea, because it has six legs but it moves on the four legs belonging to the dog or the cat.

Which animal always has its feet up in the head? The lice.

If you don't know any animal riddles, there are lots of books about riddles!

35

HOW WE MOVE AROUND

First edition for the United States and Canada
published in 2007 by Barron's Educational Series, Inc.
© Copyright 2006 by Gemser Publications, S.L.
C/Castell, 38; Teià (08329) Barcelona, Spain.
(World Rights)

Author: Núria Roca
Illustrator: Rosa M. Curto

All rights reserved. No part of this book may be
reproduced in any form, by photostat, microfilm,
xerography, or any other means, or incorporated into
any information retrieval system, electronic or
mechanical, without the written permission of
the copyright owner.

All inquiries should be addressed to:
Barron's Educational Series, Inc.
250 Wireless Boulevard
Hauppauge, NY 11788
http://www.barronseduc.com

ISBN-13: 978-0-7641-3653-5
ISBN-10: 0-7641-3653-4
Library of Congress Control Number 2006931046

Printed in China
9 8 7 6 5 4 3 2 1